I0729292

PAN AFRICAN
LIFESTYLE

Live The African Dream

The Pan African Lifestyle Blueprint

Emmanuel Bope and Solange Bope

CANADA

PAN AFRICAN LIFESTYLE INC.

Authors: Emmanuel Bope and Solange Bope

Printed and bound in Canada
First printing March 2021

Published by Pan African Lifestyle Inc.
Calgary, Alberta

ISBN 978-1-7776963-1-3 eBook

www.panafricanlifestyle.com

DEDICATION

Live The African Dream is our dedication to Pan African Lifestylers (PALs). We honour you for your embodiment of Pan-Africanism and for your daily actualization of The African Dream.

CONTENTS

FOREWORD

Before being popularly recognized as an influential Ghanaian freelance vlogger, and being named Africa's most influential YouTuber, I proudly identified myself as the village boy from Ghana – as I still do today. My journey has taken me across the beautiful continent of Africa, and has motivated my mission to encourage Pan-Africanism. My purpose is to share the beauty of all African countries, and our people, through my social platform. To my great surprise and honour, the "Africa to the world" movement has grown to an unimaginable level. Positively impacting the lives of Pan-Africans around the world, including those of the founders of Pan African Lifestyle.

I'm humbled that my effort and content have contributed to the inspiration of Pan African Lifestyle and the creation of "Live The African Dream." This book is powerful, and I too believe that when African people and the African diaspora shift their mindset, we will actualize The African Dream. Let's come together and raise the flag of the motherland. I am an African, you are also an African. Let's all be proud to be African.

Pamoja Milele!

Wode Maya

Wode Maya,

Africa's Most Influential Youtuber

PREFACE

What is Africa's biggest problem? Though this answer is subjective, and may often lead to understandable concerns surrounding leadership and the extortion and mismanagement of Africa's natural resources, we believe that there's a more pressing fundamental challenge. There's a deep-rooted problem, one deeper and richer than our fertile soils, threatening Africa's potential. That problem, which has persisted for far too long, is African people's lack of embodiment and actualization of Pan-Africanism and The African Dream.

Unsurprisingly, Africa's misrepresentation in mainstream media hasn't helped in that regard. The negative Western narrative of Africa, the impact of corruption, and the poor leadership of our nations have contributed to the misguided perception of the motherland. Western-funded coups have further plagued the continent, to where some African leaders accept the status quo and indulge in greed at the expense of Africa. Because of this environment, most of the African diaspora seemed indoctrinated and disconnected, to the point of being cynical about the future of our wonderful continent. For a long time, many African youth abroad seemed ashamed of their identity and culture. Pan-Africanism appeared impossible, and young Africans remained silent and stagnant about the potential of actualizing The African Dream.

To that notion, Nelson Mandela once said, “it always seems impossible until it's done.” All hope of connecting to Africa’s future generation seemed lost, then, Afrobeats and Afropop culture happened and shook the world by leveraging social media. The great equalizer that is the internet was the catalyst to what we believe to be the greatest cultural revolution in African history. The rise of Afropop culture on social media and the impact of Afro-influencers ignited a Pan-African renaissance – particularly within the diaspora in Europe and North America.

Who could have imagined that Afropop culture elements such as music, movies, fashion, vlogs, comedy and dance would impact the mindset of young Africans worldwide? The buzz around Black Panther, for instance, was palpable. Weeks before Ryan Coogler's fantasy African super-hero blockbuster, many in the African diaspora dressed in their African inspired costumes, lining up for the release of the film in theatres. The craze extended to social media and the engagement of black people around the world made us realize that it's possible for PALs to have collective consciousness. Especially when inspired by a wonderful vision; the possibility of a real Wakanda (The African Dream).

The film transcended cinema and transformed into a celebration of Afrocentric identity. Today, the "Wakanda Forever" salute has become an internationally recognized, and meaningful gesture, showcasing black solidarity. Though the film is fictitious, the Afrocentric energy transferred from the masterpiece is authentic. This film contributed to the impact of Afropop culture and ushered in the digital Pan-African renaissance occurring right now. Of course, our recognition of this social media phenomenon does not attempt to homogenize, stereotype, generalize, or simplify the vast history, cultures, and traditions within the motherland. Rather, our effort aims to share inspiring stories that showcase the potential and power of leveraging social media to spread Pan-Africanism and the impact it has on The African Dream. The creation of Pan African Lifestyle, and the subsequent publication of *Live The African Dream,* is a direct result of this digital Pan-African renaissance. We never witnessed such a strong cultural longing and connection among young Africans. This is why we decided to create the Pan African Lifestyle (PAL) media house and lifestyle brand.

We know and understand that Africa is the world's second-largest and second-most populated continent, hosting 1.2 billion people, representing 54 beautiful countries. We also realize that there are over 3,000 ethnic groups, who speak over 2,100 languages in all of Africa. Indeed, we are proud of the motherland's history, which spans thousands of years. Thankfully, the unpredictable impact of Afrobeats and Afropop culture, via social media, has shown that it's possible for us to transfer cultural pride to young Pan-Africans around the world. This reawakening gives social proof to Kwame Nkrumah's words: "I am not African because I was born in Africa, but because Africa was born in me." Carrying forward Nkrumah's Pan-African spirit, *Live The African Dream* is our response to the online Pan-African cultural phenomenon, and our call-to-action for PALs who love our continent as much as we do. This book refutes the divisive and indifferent perspective that cynics hold regarding the possibility of living a Pan African Lifestyle, and actualizing The African Dream in the motherland. Evidently, this book will not cure Africa of all its challenges, nor is it the only perspective. But, we live in a time like never before, and this blueprint will significantly impact Africa in the most positive way.

The internet has levelled the playing field, and Afropop artists and Pan-African social influencers have, unknowingly, shown us that African youth do care about Africa and embrace Pan-Africanism and the vision of The African Dream. Through this text, we challenge you to reconnect with your roots, express your culture, define your purpose, apply action, head home, build your legacy, and share your knowledge. It's time for you to live The African Dream.

INTRODUCTION

The rise of Pan-African influencers, platforms, and communities on social media, has made the rebirth of Pan-Africanism possible and appealing to a younger African generation. Moreover, we feel that this timely phenomenon, co-signed by African youth, has given us permission to transition Pan-Africanism into a lifestyle. In doing this, we've fused the Pan-African philosophy into a way of life that we've called the Pan African Lifestyle.

Our definition of the Pan African Lifestyle and The African Dream are straightforward. The former embodies a way of life focused on African collective consciousness and the daily actualization and enjoyment of The African Dream. In addition, the latter encapsulates the forward vision and gold-standard of Africa's highest aspirations. In short, it's the belief that all Africans, regardless of their background, can attain the highest level of success in the motherland.

If you embody Pan-Africanism and believe that The African Dream is possible, then as you read this book, the potential and power of living a Pan African Lifestyle will transition from these pages and manifest in your mind. We hope it will also actualize through your lifestyle. This book shares our experience of living a Pan African Lifestyle through eight principles that unpack the blueprint to a way of life that we believe shapes and creates the manifestation of The African Dream. *Live The African Dream* is simply the embodiment of our aspiration for all African people and the motherland. When PALs execute the blueprint principles presented in this book, the by-product of living a Pan African Lifestyle will be the achievement of The African Dream; collectively and respectively.

We hope this book has a lasting impact on the relationship Pan-Africans have with Africa and one another. This book is for all people of African descent sharing a collective mindset regarding the best interest of Africa and Africans. Though everyone can achieve principles one through five, the final three principles of the Pan African Lifestyle will only be achieved by those with the means to achieve them. The motherland requires us to come home with our best, in all aspects – particularly in terms of entrepreneurship and investment. So, in every chapter, we mention the eight principles that – when executed – will positively transform the future of Africa and our lives forever.

Now, Principle One will challenge you to transform your mindset and shift the assumptions you may have misguidedly held about Africa. The purpose here is to help you realize how your worldview or philosophy of your lifestyle can grow or ground your African Dream. Principle Two will demand you to discover your African roots. Here, you'll be presented with the importance of staying in touch with your roots. We define roots as the heritage, customs, true history, values, principles, and core tradition that make us who we are. Principle Three will encourage you to express your culture.

All people express cultural identity differently, our purpose is to inspire PALs to consciously express their Pan-African identity through their lifestyle choices. Principle Four will help you define your purpose. The reason for which you are here (your "why"). The passion that motivates you to move forward – especially through tough times. When you live in your purpose, we believe you'll experience fulfillment. Principle Five will challenge you to apply action; to execute your knowledge and actualize your African Dream.

Principle Six will dare you to head home. Summoning you to return to the land of our ancestors, and connect with the soil that is the cradle of humanity. As the roots of your Pan-African consciousness expand in the great continent, it will inspire the fruition of your future. Principle Seven outlines the importance of building a legacy. To us, this is about heritage and transferring generational wealth as we advance. Finally, Principle Eight will unpack the importance of sharing your knowledge. If you actualize these principles, you are a Pan African Lifestyler; one who embodies Pan-Africanism and actualizes The African Dream.

When PALs live by these principles, they directly manifest Pan African Lifestyle core values: unity, purpose, love, growth, culture, legacy, and happiness – that's how we will impact positive change in Africa. We become the change we envision, by living the Pan African Lifestyle and actualizing The African Dream in all that we do. Indeed, the first five principles can be achieved by all. Still, PALs will only truly complete the last three with the willpower and financial backing to significantly affect the motherland. Bear in mind that our PALs in the motherland need not to complete Principle Six given that they are already home. Meanwhile, we recommend that each PAL seeking to complete the final phase of the blueprint have solid seed capital to invest in their respective dream. Remember that only a fool tests the depth of a river with both feet.

FIRST PRINCIPLE

TRANSFORM MINDSET

Your mindset impacts your life. The mindset you hold regarding the motherland also reflects in your lifestyle – ultimately affecting how you experience your identity and culture. Your mindset permeates through your attitude and dictates how you treat others, the way you live, and the decisions you make. Therefore, in the context of Africa, the beliefs you hold in your mind make or break the potential of Pan-Africanism and the possibility of realizing The African Dream. What you do will only go as far as what you believe.

In the wise words of an African proverb, one who believes that rain is a curse has not yet met the cultivator. Though brief, this simple adage reinforces the power of perspective. In our experience, we have come to understand that our mindset changes our reality. We believe – wholeheartedly – that something as simple as transforming our mindset is the shift that will alter the future of Africa. It only takes one degree in temperature to convert water to steam.

Much like water, our mindset just needs one degree of inspiration for us to hit our boiling point. In fact, we've noticed that there are two kinds of Africans in the world, and their realities are shaped by their beliefs. One sees the potential of Africa, despite the challenges, and believes in a positive outcome for the motherland and African people. The other is cynical and only sees the worst case scenario as it relates to Africa. As Pan-Africans, we envision a borderless Africa, with established, independent countries, working together to preserve African people, culture, resources, and interest.

We believe in the collective consciousness of all people of African descent, based on our shared goal of actualizing The African Dream. Anti-Pan-Africans, however, choose to focus on problems rather than solutions. In their eyes, Pan-Africanism will never be achieved because they cannot fathom a world with people of African descent working together to achieve a shared vision, despite natural differences. So, in the context of Pan-Africanism and The African Dream, which one of these two Africans are you? The way you think about yourself and your abilities shapes your possibilities. We live by a Pan-African mindset and commit to actualize our African Dream because that's the reality we want to experience in Africa.

Shifting your mindset will change your relationship with and experience of Africa. This transformation of mind is also the first step to living a Pan African Lifestyle. Ultimately, our mindset, as it pertains to the motherland, is the deciding factor of what is possible in Africa. Because of the impact of stereotypical mainstream media propaganda, and corrupt leaders, it's understandable that some folks feel that Pan-Africanism and The African Dream is impossible. Regrettably, fixed minds equate the potential of The African Dream and Pan-Africanism with the self sabotaging behaviours of the greedy few. If all African people believe that Africa will never achieve Pan-Africanism and The African Dream, then the motherland shall remain divided and vulnerable. Alas, in this case, our people (be it in the continent or the diaspora) would be disconnected from their African culture, never to contribute their talents towards their African Dream or Africa's future.

Oppositely, when growth-oriented minds perceive and experience Pan-Africanism and the African Dream, they see and feel the vision vividly. Instead of processing things with an internal monologue, that constantly judges, using every piece of information as evidence against Pan-Africanism and The African Dream, PALs operate with a mindset that recognizes the positive incremental impact of a Pan African Lifestyle on their African Dream and on the motherland.

Our internal and external focus must not be aimed at discussing the issues of some corrupt leaders in Africa, Western interest groups, and mainstream media (that is the problem). Instead, PALs must focus on action and utilize their growth mindset to feed their ambitious appetite for solutions in the motherland. We can't transform a mindset from a fixed to growth perspective if we don't know or recognize the signs of a fixed mindset. Making this fundamental mindset shift, to see and experience our life through Pan-Africanism, is the first step to actualizing our African Dream. We can achieve anything we believe is possible in Africa.

SECOND PRINCIPLE

RECONNECT ROOTS

The strength of a tree lies within its roots. Similarly, our roots shape and strengthen us. These cultural vines are the building blocks of our dreams and continent. They connect the dots of our people and culture, bridging the gap between us and our ancestors. Therefore, knowing and cultivating your cultural roots is important because your DNA, history and heritage, is the rich soil from which you grow.

In the words of Malcom X: "Just as a tree without roots is dead, a people without history or cultural roots also become a dead people." The roots of our identity are embedded in our DNA, heritage, culture, tradition, history, and ancestry. If we choose to deny our African culture and disconnect from our motherland roots, The African Dream and Pan-Africanism will perish. Regrettably, the African identity and the expression of African culture has oftentimes been overshadowed, suppressed or disconnected. Our culture, eclipsed by the instinctual need for our people to acclimatize to the general societal construct of a Western identity, philosophy, and system; all for the sake of survival.

It's no surprise to us that the African diaspora has dealt with the challenge of acculturation; adopting foreign traditions, values, etiquette, language, and belief systems, at the risk of assimilating, to fit into the mainstream. Before the rise of Afropop culture on social media, there were few spaces from which young Africans could engage in enculturation. This was also one of our motivations for creating PAL, to foster a community whereby PALs have the opportunity to naturally enjoy the process of socialization into African culture (reconnecting to our roots). The mission was – and still is – to preserve our roots. If acculturated young Africans submerge themselves in a new culture, to the point of forgetting or losing touch with their own, then their African identity will be assimilated. Unbeknownst to us, indulging with Afropop culture, through social media, has serendipitously kept us in touch with the motherland.

Acculturation isn't necessarily bad, because it can also be a beneficial two-way process of cultural exchange. As PALs engage in various systems and cultures, they gain the opportunity to acquire and transfer new knowledge. We can all learn something good from foreign cultures and systems, but we must never lose our African heritage and identity. PALs must curate their knowledge and tap into their values and principles. Taking the best of each culture, in order to better the growth of the African Dream and our wonderful continent. In doing this, PALs reconnect with their roots and bridge the gap between Africa and the world.

Moving forward, it is beneficial for us to acknowledge the side effects of “fitting in”, as we engage the process of reconciling with our African identity. Until we recognize the damage that has been done through the Western world’s attempt to disconnect us from our history, we will be challenged by the tension between acculturation and assimilation. The Pan African Lifestyle provides a vehicle for the enculturation and socialization of our roots through a way of life that is connected to the motherland. We are proud of many PALs in the African Diaspora, who have participated in the Year of Return and leveraged DNA and ancestry testing to trace their genetic makeup and cultural roots.

Who could have imagined that a cheek swab would uproot a family lineage dating back hundreds or even thousands of years, connecting one African generation to the next. Beyond knowing where we're from, we must return to who we are. Regarding reconnecting to the motherland, there is a multitude of ways of doing so. In a general sense, we can listen to music from the continent, eat African food, and engage with other PALs around the world and in Africa. Evidently, there is a difference between consuming Afropop culture for fun and indulging in your culture because it's part of who you are. There's a difference between listening to African vibes, participating in social media challenges, going to Afro-festivals, versus transcending cultural consumption and transitioning into living a Pan African Lifestyle. Understandably, African cultural elements such as music, dance, food, comedy, and fashion are touch points by which we connect to our roots. That said, at some point, our roots must lead us home. In the famous words of Marcus Garvey: "A people without knowledge of their past history, origin and culture is like a tree without roots".

THIRD PRINCIPLE

EXPRESS CULTURE

Culture expression is a reflection of cultural perception. Our gestures, rhythm, sense of humour, language, food, lifestyle, fashion, and overall culture, are various ways by which we express our African identity. Your expression of culture, therefore, is the reflection of who you are. As you express your customs, culture, heritage, and history, you take ownership of the African narrative. Expressing your culture subconsciously empowers us all. By showcasing your Africaness, you author and authorize our culture.

Cultural identity and culture perception are a byproduct of our cultural expression and experience. As it pertains to Pan-Africanism and The African Dream, our culture and perception of reality is directly related to our expression of our African identity. The words we use, the music we vibe to, the style we display, subconsciously engineer and define the elements that form our perception and experience of The African Dream. Briefly, when we choose to express Pan-Africanism and The African Dream, the vision becomes palatable. Thus, our identity as PALs and the reality of the Pan African Lifestyle and The African Dream is a by-product of our expressive choices.

Through our expression, The African Dream can be constructed. In fact, our African identity stands because we dare to express our culture, ethnicity, nationality, customs, and Pan-Africanism. In advocating for cultural expression, we do not dispute the effects of our innate, biological influences, on our cultural identity. Instead, we hope to expose the dual impact of nurture and nature, as both build our African identity and narrative. Indeed, our DNA connects us biologically and naturally distinguishes our identity from that of others in the world. That is our natural expression of who we are. That said, our expression of our African identity also relies on our societal construct and environment – which we control. Only God controls our genetics, but we can control our narrative. Ultimately, the narrative that we express builds the reality that we experience.

To effectively influence collective consciousness and a mind shift, we must proudly showcase those elements of our culture that encourage Pan-Africanism and The African Dream. PALs worldwide can wear culturally inspiring forms of clothing and accessories to express their appreciation and connection with the motherland. Our natural hairstyles, traditional textile, dishes, humour, and our native vocabulary, among other things, are also examples of elements we ought to express in our lifestyle.

Similar to lifestyle choices such as fashion, music, dance, food, and comedy, our language expresses our culture too. Our lingo is much more than a system of communication. These dialogues that we create conveyed by speech, writing, arts and gesture, are methods by which we tell our story and express our culture. Undoubtedly, language is complexly intertwined with culture. Both influence one another in the process of expression, ultimately shaping the perception of Africa and defining what it means to be African. We wholeheartedly believe that the way in which we think about the motherland is directly influenced by our dialogue.

Through our expression, we share our values, beliefs and customs; it's the means by which our African culture and traditions are conveyed and preserved. Our tribal names, for instance, are of the highest traditional significance in the motherland, because they express a message. A name is much more than a tag that identifies. It’s a mantra that shapes one's destiny. Be it proverbial, exalting, descriptive, or otherwise, our names are an extension of us. So too is the narrative we choose to indulge in. In African culture, a name shapes one's character, establishes their social identity, and even influence their purpose. In fact, the significance of our name also impacts our mindset. That’s why we named ourselves as Pan African Lifestylers, because this name, for example, sets an expectation and an attitude that reflects a way of life that embodies Pan-Africanism and projects The African Dream. There's an intentional energy that we send out with our expression.

FOURTH PRINCIPLE

DEFINE PURPOSE

Your purpose is your definite motive for achieving a lifetime ambition that is personally meaningful. This destiny is the fundamental component of happiness, and the force driving you to achieve your African Dream. Without purpose, we live our lives with little to no meaning, focus, passion, growth and joy. Ultimately, the purpose of life is to live a life of purpose.

The significance of a life purpose is massive. Nelson Mandela once said: "There is no passion to be found playing small – in settling for a life that is less than the one you are capable of living." What we understand from Mandela's words is that there is no gain in settling for a purposeless life. Playing small is the equivalent of settling for the status quo, living a life without meaning, and diminishing your limitless potential. This is why your purpose is so important. Having a clear and deep raison d'être is no small thing. Having the courage to earnestly introspect your life's aim is daring to align your existence with your destiny.

Obviously, some of us don't want their purpose to have anything to do with Africa. Though that is regrettable, we all have freedom of choice. That said, as PALs, it's out of question for us to define our purpose without including Africa. As the premise of living The African Dream is based on actualizing our ambitions, in the motherland, through our lifestyle. Therefore, defining your purpose also aligns your destiny with Africa's future.

Your purpose should resonating with you to the core. Driving your passion to accomplish your vision, because realizing your African Dream will set you and Africa free. The reason we press the matter of defining your purpose ad nauseam is because if you do not see the destination of your journey, you will not plot the course towards it. Indeed, definiteness of purpose is the building block of your African Dream. It makes your vision so palpable that you are compelled to engineer a definite plan of action. Here lies the beauty of defining your life's chief aim; Your "why" is the motive that fuels the actualization of your African Dream.

Defining your purpose with precision is easier said then done. Even so, knowing the reason that gives your life meaning is an integral process of your lifestyle's blueprint. You must think of your success and achievements beyond material wealth and sincerely question yourself. Specify the source of your peace, expressly detail the passion that moves you. Knowing your emotional triggers, as it pertains to your areas of interests, can help you extract your mission.

You're here for a reason PAL! explaining that reason is the basis of your purpose.

An ancient African proverb says "when kings and queens lose direction, they become servants." Following this philosophy, you will surely deduce that your direction is synonymous with your purpose. So, to have dominion over your life, you must command direction. Knowing your purpose is equivalent to having a life compass - guiding life decisions, influencing behaviour, shaping goals, offering clarity and peace of mind. Purpose is being conscious of our destiny; having a state of mind that is aware of your divine assignment. You will do well to remember that consciousness is always awake, but the level of wakefulness may differ between people. The more you define your purpose, the more you heighten your level of consciousness, and embody your life meaning.

FIFTH PRINCIPLE

APPLY ACTION

One cannot plow a field by turning it over in their mind. Therefore, to achieve your aim, you must apply action.

Ideas offer innovative solutions to problems, however, ideas alone do not change the world. In fact, ideas, preparation, and even intelligence are all futile without action. Action is the initiator of momentum; the constant motion of progress. Nothing happens until a plan is put into action. That is the transitioning point between imagination and reality; Action is force. God has blessed us with the capacity to 'think' and the ability to 'do', that being said both the 'thinking' and 'doing' systems are not mutually exclusive. Some people just think, others just talk, few do. Even fewer think and execute their thoughts through strategic action.

We believe that action without deliberate thought is like a spear being throne full force in air without a target. Thus, activity that excludes thought is aimless motion. On the other hand, purpose that is strategically put into action is execution. To accomplish your African Dream, you cannot just fantasize about your vision, or be made stagnant by analysis paralysis. At some point, you'll have to bring your idea into motion; transforming your consciousness into physical energy. Moving your thoughts from the subconscious realm into the physical world. By this, we do not mean to suggest anything mysterious. Factually speaking, we are merely expressing a universal law, the first law of motion: an object will not change its motion unless a force acts on it. As it pertains to Pan-Africanism and The African Dream, if you remain at rest, unless force is applied, there will be no change in motion or direction for your future.

Ultimately, when knowledge is received, it must be structured and put into use. Otherwise, knowledge is rendered useless. Once you define your purpose and know who you are, you need to act upon your definite purpose through practical execution. Otherwise, your knowledge gained has no value. Achievement, therefore, is the by-product of the application of action towards your endgame (The African Dream). Therefore, to achieve your purpose, you must transition from inscribing your life mission in your mind, to actualizing it through your lifestyle and the achievement of your African Dream.

To act upon our beliefs and knowledge requires no crucial skill, just effort and passion (usually fuelled by an intense purpose). And so, your purpose gives you desire and reason, but your action materializes your dream. The central idea of 'living' the Pan African Lifestyle is not just a mantra, but more importantly, the constant reminder to experience The African Dream daily, through the activity we call life. Each act you make daily will magnetize your destiny and manifest the African Dream. Lest we forget, your life is a garden, if you aren't cultivating your seeds (dreams) through action, you won't harvest its fruits.

SIXTH PRINCIPLE

HEAD HOME

You will always remain a guest in a land that is not your own. Home is the constant that will always be there for you. Home is the dwelling place of your heritage, history, and freedom. Home is where your ancestors reside. Your land. No where are you better received than at home.

Once you reconnect with the motherland, you will discover that home means more than you could have ever imagined. Home is the foundation of your family tree, the dwelling place of your ancestors; the bedrock of Pan-Africanism and your African Dream. Home is where you belong. Beyond visiting the beaches, tasting the food, enjoying the landmarks, and indulging in the beautiful music and culture, the return is about healing and transformation.

Before the creation of Pan African Lifestyle, we could not conceive of The African Dream. Pan-Africanism was a distant concept that we had yet to understand. We, like many PALs in the African diaspora, were lost in the matrix of the Western world. Until we saw images of the beautiful continent, we couldn't imagine ourselves living anywhere but the West. Things changed – for the better – when the Pan-African digital renaissance occurred.

Witnessing the beauty of our landscapes, skylines, cities, and the warmth of our people, on social media, shook us to our core. The veil had suddenly been lifted from our eyes and the vision we saw was sublime. More than anything, we longed to be among our own people, to live the Pan-African way. Echoing the sentiments of Thomas Sankara: "It's the only way to live in freedom and with dignity." Home is the only place you will truly be respected, the only land where your voice is needed, the only place where your actions will affect lasting change.

Heading home is not simply a decision you make for yourself. Beyond your personal enjoyment of your natural environment, home is the safe haven of your hopes and dreams; the legacy and heritage that rightfully belongs to you and your future generation. Evidently, no home is perfect. There are challenges that come with the territory, but those temporary difficulties pale in comparison to the benefits of being in your homeland. When you're in Africa, home takes on a deeper meaning. Your home is not only defined as your birthplace, the place you are raised, or the place you settled down. More importantly, your home becomes the place from which your lineage and roots derive.

Imagine being in a place with people that look like you, a place where you won't have to explain yourself, or wonder if you fit in. A place where you will not be othered as the minority, and boxed in by a system built to enslave you. Let's be clear, you will definitely experience a phase of cultural adaptation and environmental acclimation. That said, societal adjustment is a small price to pay for freedom and self-determination. You may start from scratch, but be hopeful and best believe that Africa is the only true place on earth were anything is possible for black people. Head home and actualize the reality that is but a fantasy anywhere else in the world. Listen, though fish prosper in water does not make the sea a paradise for birds; Find where you belong and prosper in your homeland.

SEVENTH PRINCIPLE

BUILD LEGACY

As you build your legacy, you lay the foundation for your family's future and establish the ultimate contribution to the next generation. Therefore, your legacy is the fruition of seeds sown by your action, destined to become the tree that bears fruit for your children's children and for Africa.

If the average person lives to 80, all things being equal, how much time do you have to make a mark on the motherland? Mathematically speaking, 24 hours a day times 365 days a year, is 8760 hours per year. That would be 700,800 hours on this planet (without considering the leap years). Life is shorter than we think, and these numbers soberly remind us of how precious the present truly is. In retrospect, time is priceless and life is short – making what you do with your time invaluable. We ought to aspire to build legacies with the precious time that we're given. Remember, rain does not fall on one roof alone. Therefore, if others can amass incredible wealth in the world, so can you.

Naturally, we each operate under the governance of a hierarchy of needs. From physiological needs of survival, to self-actualization, each level of growth ultimately leads to the realization of The African Dream. The primary level of operation is influenced by our obligation to fulfill basic needs (food, shelter, sleep, and safety). Basic needs must be satisfied before you can attend to higher needs, those of legacy building. Those that remain in survival mode, will never enjoy the fulfillment of actualization and enlightenment. Though hardship builds character, indefinitely living in an environment of poverty only produces poverty and struggle. The motivation to surpass basic needs becomes more evident the more we struggle. Knowing this, it's imperative that you first get out of the environment of poverty, in order to master the ability to build wealth and legacy. The ultimate aspiration in achieving The African Dream is establishing generational wealth and transferable assets and knowledge.

Most people in the world generally fluctuate between basic levels of needs. This current reality is the reason we must consciously come in agreement and collaborate to inspire Pan-Africanism and actualize The African Dream in the motherland. Though it's a blessing to have shelter, food, and security, these basic needs should not be the objective for our people. Instead, we must aim for the upper echelon of abundance, in order to have the means by which to be a blessing to others. Your purpose on earth is not to survive, that is your body's primary function. When you build your legacy, you put into place structures that allow the resourcefulness of our people rather than the exploitation of our resources. When we build our legacy at home, we move forward towards innovation and development.

Though building a legacy is about establishing yourself and your future generation, through wealth transfer, never forget that building a legacy through a Pan-African lens is equally about the collective, inasmuch as it is about the individual. Therefore, wealth transfer is not only about moving financial power from your hand to your next generation, but also to your fellow Pan-African. Just as it takes a village to raise a child, it also takes a village to raise a nation's financial status. Thus, The African Dream will only prosper when our legacy building process includes group economics.

Through the proper implementation of knowledge and wealth transfer vehicles (institutions, systems, and estates), we sustain the evolution of the motherland and the continued actualization of The African Dream.

This is the grand vision of Pan African Lifestyle; the manifestation and enjoyment of the highest African aspiration in the motherland. We know that a great emphasis has been placed on wealth here, but leaving behind a notable inheritance is only half of the equation. To complete the establishment of value, we must also bequeath our history, tradition, and wisdom to the next generation. This is why a Pan African Lifestyle is important to us, because we believe your legacy is also the way of life you embody every day.

EIGHTH PRINCIPLE

SHARE KNOWLEDGE

Knowledge transfer is much more then the dissemination of information. It is the passing of the torch, imparting important wisdom, from one generation to the next. Hence, knowledge used wisely is power. But, knowledge shared is legacy.

To go fast, go alone. To go far, go together. When you transfer knowledge, you go far together. Generally, there are two main components to knowledge transfer: transfer of explicit knowledge and tacit knowledge. Explicit knowledge refers to the information that one finds in books. People that master explicit knowledge are considered book smart. Oppositely, tacit knowledge refers to information that is nuanced and gained by life experience. Those who master this kind of knowledge are street-smart. Tacit knowledge is more intangible, and the most difficult to gain and preserve. Despite their differences, both are important to establish the transfer of knowledge, wisdom and understanding.

The greatest civilizations known in human history were those that we're able to ensure a complete transfer of knowledge. One of the biggest travesties of Africa is the separation of its people and the abduction of its history, knowledge, and secrets, for everyone's benefit but Africa. We must learn from our history and ensure that our knowledge is safeguarded and transferred among our people. Those of us who acquire experience and mastery, have the responsibility to impart wisdom to others, to advance The African Dream. As we have seen through history, the motherland has been terribly disadvantaged by knowledge loss.

Much like enterprise, great nations cannot afford to lose their secrets. When PALs expose their peers to different skills and know-how, more Africans achieve The African Dream. Engaging PALs in the acquisition, and sharing of knowledge, makes Africans more ambitious and successful. Sharing knowledge pushes PALs to become better at what they do, while simultaneously pushing themselves and Africa towards excellence. Africa will be powerful when Africans choose to be resourceful and leverage resources in nature and people.

As the old saying goes, two heads are better than one. When different skills and experiences are shared, life-changing enterprises and solutions emerge. The creative energy of knowledge sharing can generate faster and more relevant solutions to the continent of Africa, particularly in this age of information. The leaders of tomorrow are among those that pursue excellence together today. Africa is only as strong as Africans, and vice versa. By sharing knowledge, PALs become the motors of Africa's innovation. There is massive skill and expertise in the African diaspora. We need to bring that back in Africa and share knowledge.

In addressing the importance of knowledge sharing, we would be remiss to omit the value of recognizing financial literacy as a form of knowledge. As you know, financial literacy is the possession of the set of skills and knowledge that allows an individual and a group to make informed and effective decisions with all of their financial resources. Given that Africa is the richest continent in the world, we would do well to master the ability to manage our finances and resources. PALs must practice group economics to establish true wealth and legacy in Africa. As Pan-Africans, we must pool our money as a collective to benefit a common interest; the actualization of The African Dream.

CONCLUSION

In opening this dialogue and creating this blueprint, we hope have echoed the sentiments of Thomas Sankara, who said: "Knowledge is not enough to change the conditions of black people. We need to create programs and systems that will empower us economically, spiritually and mentally. We need courage and action." The transformation of the motherland needs to take place within our spirit before it manifests in Africa.

Today, living a Pan African Lifestyle is our transition of Pan-Africanism into a way of life that connects Pan-Africans, and creates the catalyst for agency in the motherland. The crossover of Afropop culture on social media has given PALs a vehicle by which to spread our culture and inspire the African Dream. We have faith that PALs who execute the principles herein achieve a fulfilling life founded on seven values we hold dear: unity, purpose, love, growth, culture, legacy, and happiness. These seven life values are the core pillars and foundation of the Pan African Lifestyle.

In conclusion, the purpose of *Live The African Dream* is to convey our truth: Pan-Africanism and The African Dream are possible. To achieve this, we hope that the African diaspora around the world will: transform their mindset, reconnect with their roots, express their culture, define their purpose, apply action, head home, build a legacy, and share their knowledge. As you may know, Patrice Lumumba once said: "The day will come when history will speak. But it will not be the history which will be taught in [the Western world]. Africa will write its own history. It will be a history of glory and dignity". That prophetic day has come, Africa.

PAN AFRICAN
LIFESTYLE

GLOSSARY

Pan African Lifestyle (PAL): A way of life focused on African collective consciousness and the actualization and enjoyement of The African Dream.

The African Dream: The forward vision and standard of Africa's highest aspirations.

Pan African Lifestyler (PAL): One who embodies Pan-Africanism and actualizes The African Dream through their way of life.

Pan-Africanism: The ideology and social movement which substantiates collective collaboration of people of African descent for the advancement of Africa and African people.

PAL Principles: The PAL lifestyle blueprint which consists of seven pillars; Transform mindset, reconnect roots, express culture, define purpose, apply action, head home, build legacy, and share knowledge.

PAL Values: The seven core beliefs and core pillars; unity, purpose, love, growth, culture, legacy, and happiness.

Pan-African: One of African descent sharing a collective mindset regarding the best interest and advancement of Africa and African people.

STORY

In the summer of 2020, Emmanuel Bope and Solange Bope witnessed the impact of social media on the growth and influence of Afrobeats music, Afrodance and Afropop culture worldwide. This digital paradigm shift inspired the Congolese-Canadian couple to strategize an action plan and create a media house and lifestyle brand inspiring people of African descent to connect with their roots and take interest in the motherland. Within a few months, Emmanuel and Solange designed an apparel collection, created two card games, authored a book, and an Afropop song to push Pan African Lifestyle (PAL) through content marketing. Daily, Emmanuel and Solange reached out to Afro-influencers in hopes to generate virality for PAL. Thanks to the endorsement of popular Afro-influencers, PAL gained momentum and the brand's hype rose by the day. Pan African Lifestylers (PALs) identified with the brand's message and the buzz became a movement. Today, Pan African Lifestyle is quickly establishing itself as a household brand within the Pan-African community, inspiring the African diaspora around the world and across the motherland to live The African Dream.

Pan African Lifestyle is a media house and lifestyle brand that embodies Pan-Africanism and inspires The African Dream. We promote a way of life centered around the unity of Africa, all African people, and the achievement of the highest quality of life in the motherland. As the PAL movement and PAL Nation grow, we commit to invest in development projects in Africa. Thank you PALs, for making The African Dream possible.

www.ingramcontent.com/pod-product-compliance
Lightning Source LLC
Chambersburg PA
CBHW061223210726
48294CB00006B/1965
* 9 7 8 1 7 7 7 6 9 6 3 0 6 *